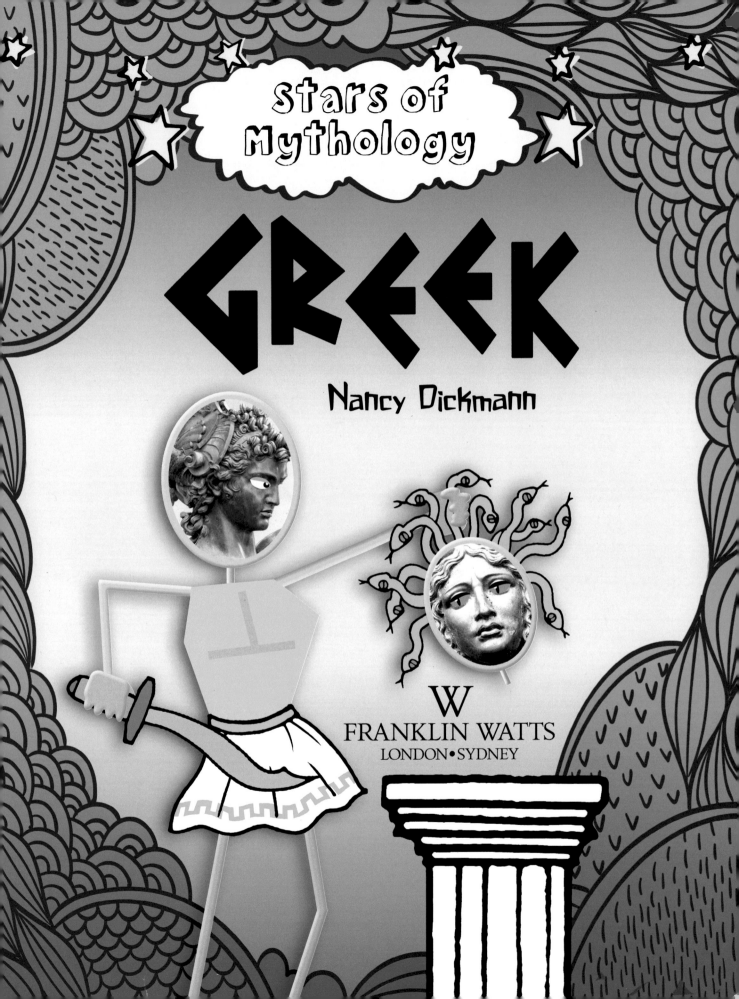

Stars of Mythology

GREEK

Nancy Dickmann

W
FRANKLIN WATTS
LONDON·SYDNEY

Franklin Watts

First published in Great Britain in 2017
by The Watts Publishing Group

Credits
Series editor: Sarah Peutrill
Series design and illustrations: Matt Lilly
Cover design: Cathryn Gilbert
Picture researcher: Diana Morris

Pic credits: abxyz/Shutterstock: front cover cr, 6c, 21b. andreiuc88/Shutterstock: 18bg, 21t. Erin Babnik/ Alamy: 14tr, 17c. Brandon Bourages/Shutterstock: 4c. csp/Shutterstock: 17t. Simon Dannhauer/Shutterstock: 8-9bg. Duncan1890/istockphoto: 10tr. EyeSeePictures/ Shutterstock: front cover c, 1c, 5t, 11c, 13cr. E Fesenko/ Shutterstock: 16b. fotojanini/istockphoto: front cover cl, 1tl, 10cl, 12bl, 13cl. Freepik: front cover bg, 1t. Kbibibi/ Freepik: 1b, 2-3, 4ca. Yuriy Kulik/Shutterstock: 19bg. Pidgorna Levgenillia/Shutterstock: 20c. Matt Lilly: 12br, 17b. Luxerendering/Shutterstock: 7bg. Musée Thomas Dobrée, Nantes/Gianai D'Agli Orti/The Art Archive: 23c, 24tr, 25t, 25b. Stefano Paterno/Alamy: 15c, 16cr. Radiokafka/Dreamstime: 14bl, 16bl, 17tr. Samot/ Shutterstock: 4b. Josef Skacel/Shutterstock: 14-15bg. Torsten Stahlberg/istockphoto: 5b, 26, 28b. Alex Tois/ Shutterstock: 27c, 29tr. Jorden Udvang/istockphoto: 3t, 27tr, 28t, 29tc. Haris Vythoulkas/Shutterstock: 22c, 24tl, 24b, 31b. CC Wikimedia: 7c, 8t, 9t, 18c, 19c, 21tl.

Every attempt has been made to clear copyright. Should there be any inadvertent omission please apply to the publisher for rectification.

HB ISBN: 978 1 4451 5158 8
PB ISBN: 978 1 4451 5157 1

Printed in China

Franklin Watts
An imprint of
Hachette Children's Group
Part of The Watts Publishing Group
Carmelite House
50 Victoria Embankment
London EC4Y 0DZ

An Hachette UK Company
www.hachette.co.uk
www.franklinwatts.co.uk

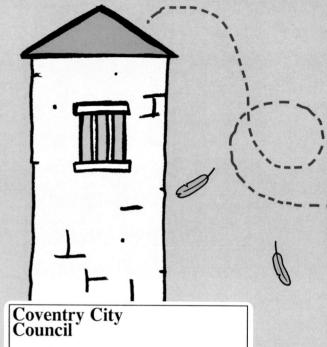

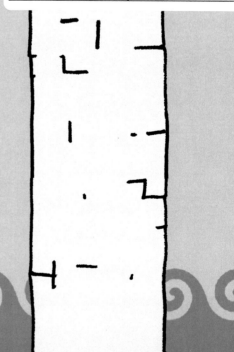

Contents

Greek mythology

Thousands of years ago, an amazing civilisation flourished in the land that is now Greece. The ancient Greeks built cities, temples and ships. They fought wars and traded across the Mediterranean Sea, spreading their culture far and wide. Their culture included sculpture, pottery, sport and story-telling, especially myths. Some myths were an attempt to explain why the world was the way it was, and others were a way of remembering historical events. The myths can also stand on their own as fascinating stories.

Gods and goddesses

The Greeks believed in a wide range of gods and goddesses, and many of the myths are about these characters. Each god or goddess was linked to a particular aspect of life. For example, Poseidon was the god of the sea, and Aphrodite was the goddess of love. The gods sometimes came down from their home, Mount Olympus, to walk among ordinary people (the mortals), and they quarrelled and schemed and fell in love with each other, just like people do. The Greeks believed that the gods could affect their daily life, so they worked hard to keep them happy by building temples and offering sacrifices.

Poseidon, god of the sea

Who's who?

It wasn't just gods and goddesses who featured in Greek myths. There was a whole host of other characters, including lesser spirits like nymphs and satyrs. There were demigods, who were the children of a god or goddess and a mortal. There were also mortal heroes such as Jason and Odysseus, who had exciting adventures. Some of the stories feature monsters and creatures such as centaurs, cyclops and chimaras.

The women in the stories were often treated like property. This reflected their place in society at the time – confined to the home and not treated equally. They had to follow the will of their father or husband.

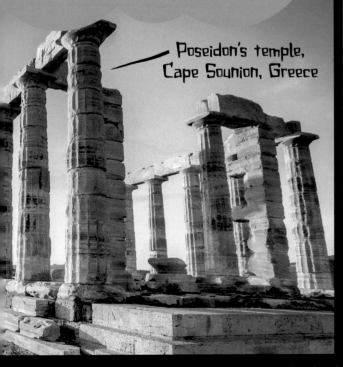

Poseidon's temple, Cape Sounion, Greece

How do we know?

For centuries, the myths weren't written down. Instead, they were passed from one person to another as part of an oral tradition. Poets called bards recited myths to audiences. The stories often changed slightly the more they were told, and for many of them there are different versions. They started to be written down in around 800 BCE.

It's not easy memorising poems that are thousands of lines long. So if I forget the words, I just make it up. Who'll notice?

Bard

Zeus and Europa

Read their story on pages 8–9.

Fact file: Zeus

Zeus was the god of thunder and the sky. After overthrowing his father, Cronus, he became the undisputed king of the gods. He ruled the world from the snow-covered peak of Mount Olympus, and occasionally sent thunderbolts down to earth to punish the unworthy.

Zeus married his sister, Hera, and became the father of other important gods such as Ares (god of war) and Athena (goddess of wisdom). He also had many other children with nymphs and mortal women. Europa was just one of Zeus' many love interests.

Zeus in his own words

Powers:
I can change into several different animals, or even a shower of gold (girls love it!). Plus I can control the weather, and my thunderbolt is pretty ace for smiting.

My parents:
Cronus and Rhea. (Don't ask me about my dad – we have a few issues.)

Crowning achievements:
Overthrowing my father and taking over the world, and keeping my affairs secret from my wife.

Children:
Too many to count. What can I say – I have a weakness for the ladies!

Not to be confused with:
My brother Poseidon. Or Hades. Or any other god, to be honest! (Did I mention Poseidon?)

Fact file: Europa

Europa was a princess from Phoenicia, an ancient civilisation in the land that is now Israel, Syria and Lebanon. Her father, Agenor, was King of Tyre, an important coastal city. In some versions of the story her mother is called Telephassa, and in others she is called Argiope.

After her adventure with Zeus (see pages 8–9), Europa stayed in Crete, where she had three sons. One of them was Minos, who ordered the building of the famous labyrinth (see pages 15–17). She later married Asterion, King of Crete.

Europa in her own words

My family:
I've got three brothers — Cadmus, Cilix and Phoenix. Cadmus is a real pain. He thinks he's some sort of hero and that I need his constant protection. Yeah, whatever, Cadmus!

My hobbies:
Going to the beach with my girlfriends, picking flowers, doing the princess thing.

Things that make me go OMG:
Cute animals. Can't get enough of them!

I wish I were better at:
Swimming.

7

Swept away ... Cadmus' story

My sister Europa is such a moron. I mean, I love her – obviously – but sometimes she does the dumbest things.

Like last week, for example. She and a bunch of her friends had gone down to the beach to pick flowers and do girly things. They were out for ages and Mum said, 'Cadmus, you'd better go and find her.'

So I set off, and when I came around the headland I could see them all down on the sand. There was a white bull with them, and the girls were going mental. Not like they were scared – you should have seen them fawning over it! I mean, as bulls go, it was all right, but all it made me think of was dinner.

The girls were patting it, and hanging garlands of flowers around its horns. And the bull was lapping up all the attention. It knelt down in front of Europa, like it wanted her to get on its back.

Now, this was where I got suspicious. Everyone knows that Zeus has to disguise himself in all sorts of ways so that his wife, Hera, doesn't catch him cheating on her. Strolling up to some lush young maiden in the form of a bull is just the sort of thing he'd try.

But Europa didn't stop to think. She was totally loving it. She climbed up on his back and before you could blink, the bull had run into the water and started swimming away.

Help!!!

Europa is a princess, so she knows how to do things like weave, and dance and sing and all sorts. But she can't swim. And as the bull swam further and further out to sea, I could see the panicked look in her eyes. I was already running down to the beach, but I knew it was too late. I got there in time to see a tiny speck disappearing over the horizon, towards Crete.

So now my parents can't stop crying and Europa's sailed off to this amazing island to be the queen of a god.

On second thoughts, maybe she's not so dumb after all!

Perseus and Medusa

Read their story on pages 12–13.

Fact file: Perseus

The beautiful princess Danae had been locked away in a bronze tower by her father, King Acrisius. Zeus came to her as a shower of gold, leaving her pregnant. She had a son, **Perseus**. Acrisius was furious, and locked both mother and baby into a chest and threw it into the sea.

They were rescued, and Perseus grew up in the court of Polydectes. After the encounter with Medusa (see page 12), Perseus rescued the princess Andromeda (right) from being sacrificed to a sea monster, and married her.

Perseus in his own words

Greatest strengths:
I'm pretty good with a sword. And being the son of Zeus gives me a certain something.

Weirdest relative:
My grandfather Acrisius. A prophet told him that his grandson (that's me!) would kill him. To be honest, the thought probably would never have crossed my mind, but then he did try to kill me as a baby, so who knows?

Things I can't stand:
Squishy eyeballs, and creepy kings who want to marry

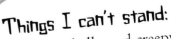

Fact file: Medusa

Medusa and her two sisters, Stheno and Euryale, were known as the Gorgons. Some legends say that all three sisters had sharp fangs, brass claws and hideous faces. They had the power to turn people to stone just by looking at them.

One legend says that Medusa was once a gorgeous young woman. The sea god, Poseidon, was so taken by her beautiful hair that he seduced her in one of Athena's temples. Athena was furious, and she turned Medusa's hair into snakes in revenge.

Medusa in her own words

Life's so unfair, volume 1:
So I went out with Poseidon, okay, because who could turn down a god? Not this girl! But he gets off scot-free, and I'm the one who's punished.

Silver lining:
A nest of snakes turns out to be a pretty low-maintenance hairstyle.

Not-so-silver lining:
My sisters are the only ones who can see me without turning to stone, so my social life is pretty dull.

Life's so unfair, volume 2:
My two sisters are immortal, but I'm not. I can see how this might end badly one day!

Diary of a hero ... by Perseus

2ND DAY AFTER THE RISING OF ORION✲:

I can totally tell that Polydectes is hot for my mother, and would love to get me out of his way so he can force her to marry him. Today we got an invitation to a big party he's throwing, and guess what everyone is supposed to bring as a gift? A horse! Where am I supposed to get the money for that? I'll just have to tell him to stuff it.

4TH DAY AFTER THE RISING OF ORION:

Well, that went even worse than I thought it would. Polydectes was furious that I hadn't brought a gift. He wouldn't let it drop, and I finally said I'd bring him anything he wanted, just to get him off my back. Then he smiles this evil smile and tells me to bring him the head of Medusa. You know, the Gorgon who can turn men to stone just by looking at them! So no trouble there, then.

3RD DAY AFTER THE SETTING OF AQUILA:

I've been searching for Medusa for weeks now, and last night I finally had a breakthrough. A man and a woman came up to my camp in the forest – it was Hermes and Athena! They lent me a shield, a magic sickle and winged sandals to help me in my quest.

Polydectes

7TH DAY AFTER THE SETTING OF AQUILA:

Today was dead weird. I visited these three disgusting old women who share a single eyeball, passing it back and forth. I snatched it (totally gross and squishy, btw) until they told me how to find Medusa. And now I've got a helmet that makes me invisible!

2ND DAY AFTER THE RISING OF LEO:

What a day! I found Medusa in her lair and used the reflection in the shield to look at her without being turned to stone. Even if you ignore the snakes, she is pretty hideous! The invisibility helmet let me sneak up on her, and one swipe of the magic sickle took her head off. But even though she's dead, the head is still dangerous. I think I'll keep it — it may come in useful with Polydectes!

Ugh!

✿Greek calendars used cycles of the moon and sun and also the stars to affix dates.

Theseus and Ariadne

Read their story on pages 16–17.

Fact file: Theseus

The Greek hero **Theseus** was raised by his mother before going on a journey to find his father. Along the way, he fought and killed many of the bandits who had been terrorising travellers.

Every so often Athens had to send its bravest young men and most beautiful women to be sacrificed to the Minotaur, who was half man and half bull. One year Theseus volunteered to go, and he succeeded in killing the Minotaur. He later ruled Athens as king.

Theseus in his own words

My parents:

Officially, King Aegeus and Queen Aethra. But there are rumours that the sea god Poseidon is my real father. It would certainly explain my amazing skills!

Villains I've killed:

Periphetes the Club Bearer, Cercyon the Wrestler, the Minotaur, obviously. Oh, and the one who kicked people off cliffs – I can never remember his name!

Don't remind me about:

That time I forgot to hoist a white sail on the way back from Crete, to signal to my father that I was still alive. He was so depressed that he threw himself into the sea!

Fact file: Ariadne

Ariadne was the daughter of King Minos of Crete. She was put in charge of the labyrinth where the Minotaur – who was her half-brother – was kept. When she fell in love with Theseus at first sight, she was in the perfect position to help him find and kill the Minotaur.

After fleeing Crete with Theseus, he abandoned her on the island of Naxos. She later married Dionysos, the god of wine. In some versions of the story she either hangs herself, or is killed by the goddess Artemis or the hero Perseus.

Ariadne in her own words

My parents:
King Minos and Queen Pasiphae.

My homeland:
Knossos, Crete – and I miss it.

Greatest skill:
I can find my way through the labyrinth with my eyes closed.

My biggest regret:
Agreeing to help that idiot Theseus. As if it wasn't bad enough that he killed my brother, he sailed off in the middle of the night without me!

Royally dumped

In our exclusive story, we can reveal that the newly-crowned King of Athens is not above using women to advance his own career – and then cutting and running.

Eagle-eyed observers have spotted the lovely Ariadne on the island of Naxos – looking fabulous but WITHOUT Theseus, the Athenian prince she ran off with not long ago. When last seen they were sailing from Crete, madly in love. So what went wrong?

LOVE AT FIRST SIGHT

Theseus had arrived in Crete as part of the annual consignment of hot young Athenian men, doomed to be sacrificed to the bloodthirsty Minotaur. But he caught the eye of a certain princess, who decided to risk everything for him.

'When I saw him getting off the ship, I went weak at the knees,' Ariadne confided to a close friend at the time. 'He was gorgeous – I couldn't just let him get eaten by the Minotaur.'

Secret of his success

The princess gave Theseus a sword and a jewelled cord to make sure he didn't get lost in the labyrinth. But this gave him an unfair advantage, according to the other Athenian men sent to face the Minotaur. 'Everyone makes Theseus out to be this great hero,' said one, who didn't want to be named. 'But he never could have killed the Minotaur without Ariadne's help.'

Time for an upgrade

At any rate, it looks like Ariadne may have already moved on. 'Ariadne was really upset about the whole Theseus thing at first, but she's totally over it now,' says a source close to the princess. 'Theseus was just a mortal, but her new boyfriend, Dionysos — he's an actual god!'

Suicide scandal

Athens is still reeling from the shock suicide of King Aegeus. Rumours are swirling that Theseus forgot the pre-arranged signal to show that he was safe: changing his ship's black sails to white. 'It just goes to show you what a stupid decision it was to dump Ariadne,' revealed a friend of the princess. 'She would have remembered to change the sails — she's good at details like that.'

AAAAAAHHGH!

Hades and Persephone

Read their story on pages 20–21.

Fact file: Hades

Hades was the brother of Zeus. As a baby, he was swallowed by his father, Cronus, along with their other siblings. Zeus forced Cronus to vomit them all up, and then Hades joined Zeus in the struggle to overthrow Cronus and the other Titans.

After their victory, Zeus, Hades and Poseidon drew straws to divide up the world between themselves. Zeus got the sky, Poseidon got the sea and Hades ended up with the Underworld, where the souls of the dead end up.

Hades in his own words

My home:
The Underworld, land of the dead. It's not the cheeriest place, but needs must. At least I got to name it after myself!

Unluckiest moment:
Drawing the short straw that day with my brothers, and ending up here. (I still think Poseidon must have cheated.)

Coolest kit:
I have a helmet that makes me invisible.

What makes me mad:
Dead people trying to leave the Underworld, or alive ones trying to come in to steal souls.

Fact file: Persephone

Persephone was the daughter of Zeus and his sister Demeter, goddess of the harvest. She was a beautiful young woman, and most of the gods wanted to marry her, offering fabulous gifts in exchange for her hand.

To protect her daughter from suitors, Demeter took her away to live in secrecy. But she was kept busy making sure that the crops grew well, so she couldn't guard Persephone all the time. Hades took advantage of this and one day arrived in his chariot to kidnap her.

Persephone in her own words

My family:
Totally screwed up! My dad is my mum's brother, and now I've been forced to marry my uncle. Everyone says that we're immortals and that's just how we roll, but still – ugh.

What I love:
Being out in nature. It sounds lame, but helping plants grow is actually pretty rewarding.

I'm really good at:
Counting. In particular, counting the days until I can leave this underground dump and go back up into the sun again.

Favourite foods:
Anything but pomegranate!

Phew, what a famine!

Negotiations have stalled in the ongoing campaign to stop the famine that has been ravaging the country for months — and a simple pomegranate seed appears to be the source of the problem.

We last reported that the goddess Demeter is to blame for the failure of the harvest. Angry at the kidnapping of her daughter Persephone, she went on strike from her job of helping crops grow. A highly-placed source tells us that the kidnapper was none other than Hades. 'Hades has been looking for a bride for years, but there weren't any takers,' said our source. 'Who wants to be a queen if you have to live in a dank and gloomy underground palace?'

A few weeks ago Demeter was spotted on her way to Mount Olympus to meet with Zeus behind closed doors, and later gave a brief statement. 'I'm pleased to report that Zeus now agrees that my daughter's kidnapping was illegal,' a relieved-looking Demeter said. 'He's already sent Hermes to collect Persephone from the Underworld.'

With Demeter busy looking for her daughter, the crops in the fields have withered and died.

Hades tempted Persephone with a pomegranate seed.

But the loving mother's triumph was short-lived. A visibly distressed Hermes soon returned, but refused to comment as he flew off to fetch Zeus. Our source tells us that Hades had apparently tricked the princess into eating a pomegranate seed, knowing that anyone who eats something in the Underworld – even the tiniest crumb – can never leave.

Experts say that now Zeus is involved, the options on the table will include a time-sharing deal in which Persephone can spend half of the year with her mother, and the other half with Hades. Demeter would have to agree to only go on strike when Persephone is in the Underworld, giving farmers a six-month growing season.

'It would be better than nothing, I suppose,' said a local farmer. 'But Zeus has definitely got to sort this out if he wants people to keep worshipping him.'

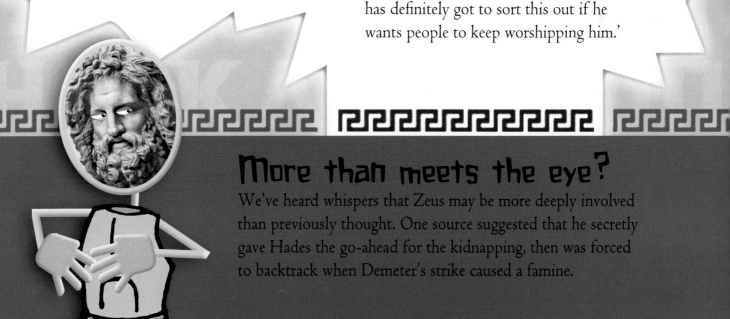

More than meets the eye?

We've heard whispers that Zeus may be more deeply involved than previously thought. One source suggested that he secretly gave Hades the go-ahead for the kidnapping, then was forced to backtrack when Demeter's strike caused a famine.

Athena and Arachne

☆ Read their story on pages 24–25.

Fact file: Athena

Athena was the daughter of Zeus and Metis. Zeus swallowed Metis while she was still pregnant, worried that her child would overthrow him, in the same way that Zeus had beaten his own father. But Athena sprang from his forehead, fully grown and wearing armour.

Athena was the goddess of wisdom, as well as war and crafts such as weaving. She never married or had children, but she became the patron goddess of Athens.

Athena in her own words

My family:
My dad, Zeus, may have swallowed my mother, but he's a sweetie really. He lets me play with his thunderbolts sometimes.

Views on mortals:
Most of them aren't so bad. I've given them skills like cooking and sewing, and sometimes I help them with their quests.

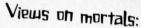

Coolest kit:
My armour. Perseus gave me the head of Medusa, and I put it on my armour.

What makes me mad:
I'm the goddess of justice as well as wisdom, so I can't just fly off the handle at any old thing. But I don't like mortals thinking that they're better than me.

Fact file: Arachne

Arachne was an ordinary mortal girl. In some versions of the story she is the daughter of Idmon, a cloth dyer, and grew up in the village of Hypaepa. She was extremely talented at weaving cloth, and she became famous for her skill.

When Athena heard about a girl who claimed to be a better weaver than she was, she became angry. The two women had a weaving contest, and even Athena was amazed at Arachne's skill. But in anger, she turned the girl into a spider.

Arachne in her own words

Career goal:
To be the best weaver in the world, full stop.

Views on gods:
They're no better than people, really! You wouldn't believe some of the stories about what they get up to.

Greatest weakness:
Most people would say it's over-confidence. But I think that's actually a strength, don't you? I say, if you've got it, flaunt it!

War of the weavers

Athena

Everyone's been talking about the recent weaving contest between Athena and Arachne, which ended with the goddess using her powers to turn her rival into a spider. We've managed to get the first exclusive interview with Athena.

So was it a tragic over-reaction, or a justified punishment? You decide!

Arachne

INTERVIEWER: What made you decide to challenge Arachne to a duel?

ATHENA: I don't know where you heard that. *She's* the one who challenged *me!*

INTERVIEWER: Don't you think it was unfair for a powerful goddess to take on a mortal?

ATHENA: Let me put it another way. Don't *you* think it was disrespectful for a mere girl to boast about being a better weaver than *me?* I gave her a chance to take it back – I even disguised myself as a crippled old woman so that she wouldn't feel intimidated.

INTERVIEWER: Tell us how the contest went down.

ATHENA: Well, Arachne was surprised when I revealed myself in my true form, but she got straight to work. You should have seen her fingers fly!

She'll never recognise me!

I conjured up a loom and started too, and I decided to weave a scene with a message. It showed me with my family on our thrones on Mount Olympus, and around the edges I wove scenes of people who had defied the gods and been punished for it.

INTERVIEWER:
Was that meant to be a warning?

ATHENA: Well, duh. What do you think?

INTERVIEWER:
What happened next?

ATHENA: I took a break to look over at Arachne's loom, and I couldn't believe what I saw! She was weaving scenes of the gods making fools of themselves by chasing after mortal girls. Even my own father, Zeus! Her technique was amazing, I'll grant you that, but it was so disrespectful that I just snapped.

I want to be the best weaver in the world!

EEK!

INTERVIEWER:
And that's when you turned Arachne into a spider?

ATHENA: Well, yes. But she deserved it! Now she can weave webs all day long, but no one will shower praise on her. And if she still boasts about being a better weaver than me ... well, spiders often get stepped on, if you catch my meaning ...

Daedalus and Icarus

Read their story on pages 28–29.

Fact file: Daedalus

Daedalus was a famous inventor and artist. King Minos of Crete hired him to design a labyrinth that could hold the fearsome Minotaur. When it was finished, Minos worried that Daedalus would share the secret of the labyrinth, so he locked him in a tower.

Daedalus made wings out of feathers and wax to escape, for both him and his son, Icarus.

Daedalus in his own words

Most ungrateful customer:
I built Minos a brilliant labyrinth, but he locked me up! I would never tell anyone how to get in or out — in fact, I got lost in there once myself!

Knottiest problem solved:
I ran a string through a spiral seashell by tying it to an ant, then luring it into the shell with a drop of honey. The ant did all the work.

Biggest worry:
My son Icarus is a clever boy, but he doesn't always think about what he's doing. One day it'll get him into trouble.

Fact file: Icarus

Icarus was imprisoned with his father. Before they set off to escape, Daedalus gave Icarus two warnings: don't fly too high, in case the sun melts the wax; and don't fly too low, in case the spray from the sea wets the feathers and makes them too heavy.

Icarus in his own words

My family:
My dad is a bit of a mad scientist, always coming up with crazy new inventions. I give him a hand with them sometimes.

What I can't stand:
Being cooped up. Especially in a tower with only one window.

A perfect day out:
Anything where I can go fast — on horseback, in a chariot, or whatever. Life's too short to go slow!

Biggest weakness:
My dad says that I never listen. I don't know what he's on about — I must have been listening to have heard that!

Air crash horror

Reports of strange flying creatures have been flooding in from all across the Aegean Sea. Were they men or beasts?

Our reporters have travelled throughout the region to find out.

The earliest sightings were on the island of Crete, near Knossos. Giorgios, a local fisherman, reported seeing two figures low in the sky, just after midday. 'They looked like men, but they had wings like an eagle,' he said.

'Yeah, but you had been sitting out in the sun for several hours at that point,' his wife was quick to point out.

STOP FUSSING DAD!

BE CAREFUL SON!

Despite her doubts, another fisherman, Stavros, was able to back up Giorgios' story, and offered another tantalising clue. 'I went past the palace earlier. You know the tower where the king has that inventor locked up? What's his name – Daedalus or something? Well, there was an old man and a boy on the roof of the tower. I couldn't see what they were doing, but the old man was saying something about not going too high.'

ICARUS! ICARUS!

A source at the palace confirmed that Daedalus and his son, Icarus, did indeed escape from their cell this morning. An eyewitness on Naxos later spotted two human-shaped figures flying through the sky. 'One of them was flying nice and straight,' she told us. 'The other one was going faster and flying much higher, doing loop-the-loops and all sorts.' She then showed us something she found nearby: a small clump of bird's feathers, held together with what looked like beeswax.

The most chilling report came from a farmer on the island of Patmos. 'When they passed overhead, the young one was going higher and higher – I could hear him laughing. But even from down here I could see that his wings were coming apart. The old man kept shouting after him, "Icarus! Icarus!" And then he just dropped like a stone into the sea and died. It was horrible.'

OOPS!

We finally caught up with a distraught Daedalus at the court of King Cocalus, on Sicily. 'I told him a hundred times that the wax would melt if he went too close to the sun,' he said. 'But teenage boys never listen.'

Glossary

court the family, supporters and servants of a king or other ruler

demigod a person who is semi-divine, such as the child of a god and a mortal

famine when there is little or no food available for many people

Gorgon one of three sisters who had live snakes instead of hair, and who could turn anyone who looked at them into stone

immortal living forever and never dying or decaying. The gods and goddesses of Ancient Greece were immortal.

labyrinth a complicated life-size maze in Crete that was built to house the fearsome Minotaur

loom a wooden frame used for weaving thread into cloth

Minotaur a creature with the body of a man and the head of a bull, who lived in the Labyrinth

mortal an ordinary person who will eventually die instead of living forever

myth a traditional story that tries to explain why the world is the way that it is, or to recount legendary events

nymph a nature spirit often pictured as a beautiful woman living in a river or forest

oral tradition the passing on of literature and culture by word of mouth from one person to another, rather than being written down

pomegranate fruit of the pomegranate tree with many seeds

prophet a person who can predict what will happen in the future

recite to say something from memory out loud to an audience

sacrifice to give a gift to the gods, such as food or slaughtered animals.

sickle a farming tool with a curved blade that is used for cutting corn and other plants

smite to hit someone with a weapon or hand

strike to refuse to work as a protest against unfair conditions

temple building devoted to the worship of one or more gods

Titans the older generation of Greek gods who were overthrown by Zeus and his siblings

Underworld the place where Greeks believed that souls went after they died, imagined as being a gloomy underground realm

Books

☆

Ancient Greece (Discover through Craft),
Anita Ganeri, Franklin Watts

The Orchard Book of Greek Myths,
Geraldine McCaughrean, Orchard Books

Ancient Greece (The History Detective Investigates),
Rachel Minay, Wayland

A Visitor's Guide to Ancient Greece (Usborne Visitor Guides),
Lesley Sims, Usborne Publishing

Greek Myths (Stories From Around the World),
Anna Claybourne and Fiona Sansom, Franklin Watts

Websites

Find out about the gods, goddesses and heroes of Greek myth at this website:
www.greekmythology.com

Read some of the more terrifying tales from ancient Greece here:
www.ngkids.co.uk/history/Greek-Myths

Go here to find out more about religion in ancient Greece:
www.bbc.co.uk/guides/zgt7mp3

Note to parents and teachers: Every effort has been made by the Publishers to ensure that these websites are suitable for children, that they are of the highest educational value, and that they contain no inappropriate or offensive material. However, because of the nature of the Internet, it is impossible to guarantee that the contents of these sites will not be altered. We strongly advise that Internet access is supervised by a responsible adult.

Index

These are the lists of contents for
each title in Stars of Mythology.

Chinese
Chinese mythology

Huangdi and Chiyou • Clash of the gods

Yi and Chang'e • Gone girl

Da Yu and Nujiao • A slight misunderstanding

Gao Xin and Pan Hu • Man's best friend

Zhinu and Niulang • Magpie mystery solved!

Monkey and the jade emperor • The peach thief

Indian
Hindu mythologyy

Krishna and Kamsa • Wrestling for revenge

Savitri and Satyavan • Love conquers all

Rama and Sita • Wedding of the year

Hanuman and Ravana • Monkey mayhem

Parvati and Ganesha • How Ganesha got his head

Hiranyakashyap and Prahlada • Not so immortal after all

Egyptian
Egyptian mythology

Osiris and Set • Sibling tivalry (Set's diary)

Isis and Ra • Ra's secret name ... revealed?

Tefnut and Thoth • Tefnut's tantrum

Anubis and Ammut • Welcome to the underworld

Hathor and Sekhmet • The sun god speaks

Thutmose and Horus • The prince's dream (a worker's tale)

Roman
Roman mythology

Dido and Aeneas • All for love

Romulus and Remus • A shepherd's diary

Juno and Vulcan • The golden throne

Castor and Pollux • Family feud

Hercules and Atlas • Tricked!

Jupiter and Baucis • Unexpected guests

Greek
Greek mythology

Zeus and Europa • Swept away

Perseus and Medusa • Diary of a hero

Theseus and Ariadne • Royally dumped

Hades and Persephone • Phew, what a famine!

Athena and Arachne • War of the weavers

Daedalus and Icarus • Air crash horror

Viking
Norse mythology

Odin and Baugi • A letter to Suttung

Skadi and Njord • Worst day ever

Tyr and Fenrir • When good pets go bad

Thor and Loki • Wedding mayhem

Freyr and Gerd • Playing hard to get

Frigg and Baldur • A mother's love